louder

louder

Kerrin P. Sharpe

Victoria University Press

VICTORIA UNIVERSITY PRESS
Victoria University of Wellington
PO Box 600 Wellington
vup.victoria.ac.nz

Copyright © Kerrin P. Sharpe 2018
First published 2018

A catalogue record is available at the National Library of New Zealand

ISBN 9781776561964

Printed by Ligare, Auckland

for my husband, Gordon Davidson

Contents

beyond the wire

endangered

refugee

what we hear

where will the fish sleep?

flames of faces in the rainforest

why does all that smoke look like snow?

when we flew past the chimneys
stars of ash clung to our legs

soldiers stole their paintings
and loaded their families
into trains

a nursing elephant in West Bengal
is shot and maimed as she drinks

eaten by manacles
drowning again and again

calves stumble
into scopes

boys who never escape
the sudden collapse
of tonnes of metal

no one looks for us
we cannot see the sun

louder

here no one keeps company
with the Roma

the barber recognises surrender
how it stretches its neck in sunlight
how it closes its eyes like a blade

beyond the wire

louder

elephants paint their faces
to restore themselves

adding tusks where poachers
took their ivory

these artists use soft sable
brushes made in the Congo

and paint their parents
bathing in rivers

crossing Ugandan borders
or even birthing
when hunters arrive

and if you can imagine
thousands of elephants
all in outdoor studios

painting themselves and their tribe
as whole elephants

even as guns are raised
and calves stumble
into scopes even as

trunks and heads are mutilated
their painting continues
louder than bullets

when the barber talks about elephants

the barber's shop boasts elephant
fezzes tea towels photographs
cigar cases shaving mugs
never ivory and he croons elephant songs
swinging his scissors from side to side

the barber believes wild elephants
stray into cities because they remember
when the jungle went on forever
and convinced the crowds are thieves
they plunge into marketplaces plunder cars
in search of vegetation

on the world page of the morning paper
a customs officer is cataloguing tusks
like census exhibits and the thought of these elephants
makes the barber bury his razor
even now as his scissors charge a young man's hair

a nursing elephant in West Bengal
is shot as she drinks
from a river
and her baby feeds until
her mother freezes under the Indian sun

Kaimanawa song

codas of horses
are adrift

songs of ancestry
songs of leaving
a waiata of grassland

April horses
in foal horses
with foals yearlings
older horses

in rimu
in tōtara

when the trucks tumble tussock
when the trucks sweep the forest

the leafy pockets
of mataī and kāmahi
are not deep enough
to hide the horses

among the flurry
of manes and hooves
the rage of Tāne

the ship breakers

in the field of the sea
cables of boys dissect
the bones and skull
of a cargo ship

boys small enough to squeeze
inside smokestacks and fill
the stomachs of the steel
rerolling mills boys who don't

feel shards of asbestos
or paint settle in their lungs
or smell gas that takes their brothers
and lights the faces of rice-fish

boys who never escape
the sudden collapse
of tons of metal
boys who hear at high tide

water in the folds of the hull
chant the names
of their dead brothers

talking back to old masters

inside your paintings
of rammed smouldering ships
there are rowers
as cold as diamonds

my son built a cutaway
slave ship from balsam wood
the oars toothpicks
from the new world

one night fast awake
the ship rowed round his room
he heard slanted oars
slashing his shelves of maritime history

by morning the sea had run
away with the slaves
the carpet surged
and rumpled like canvas

Roma @ Marble Arch

I surface from the long low
tunnels where light turns
from the Roma

all day I play violin
to men with Rolex watches
to women in Prada coats
no one gives to the Roma

at home in Sibhi
whenever I played
Gypsy Melody my horse
would leave the fire

to dance with my wife
here no one keeps company
with the Roma

at night in my cardboard bed
I hear in the overhead
escalators the hooves
of Romania

I hear my horse bringing me
a bucket of pure air
over the Transylvanian Alps
over all those fields

she has days when she's back

she has days when she's back
in a Tokyo laundry
feeding the mangle
enough white sheets
for the Feast of the Dead

days with the chance
to free the world's insects
from one hundred
detachable collars

days when it took
hours to fold pillowslips
into lanterns
for huge hotel beds

days when there was a difference
between a laundered dove
and a sparrow laid out in snow

why does all that smoke look like snow?

smoke settles like hair over Shanxi
the workers pull tricycles to and from
the power plant
why does all that smoke look like snow?

each time the barber coughs
his lungs rattle like wild swans
and when he inhales
he hears the voices

of his ancestors like his uncle
who lost his breath
picking rocks from low-cost coal
miners who are tight for time visit the barber

for no-nonsense cuts and shaves
hot water returns them to the world
and he shoots the breeze with them
while their hair surrenders

to the laws of blades
this morning on the snowy threshold
of his shop the barber finds
the body of a smoky wren

his helmet feathers so close
to the wood of his tiny skull
he'd never need a haircut
the barber lays him out

on the shop's brazier
and thinks about burial balloons
where human ashes are sent
high in the air only to fall like miners

into the smoke of Shanxi

from the barber on the bridge

from the barber on the bridge
the groom wants the sharpest shave
no strop no blood
no tales from Antigua

the barber keeps his other eye
on the bride in the boatshed
steaming the groom's panama
his blazer his flannels

the barber recognises surrender
how it stretches its neck in sunlight
how it closes its eyes like a blade

the groom never mentions his bride
or what's about to happen

when the wedding gondola arrives
with prow of canna lilies
the groom shouts at the bride

and runs down to the boatshed
where she dresses him
with the same silence

the unpaid barber
washes his razor

pit pony

was there soft music?

were the lights low?

did she show the moon her son?

was there a contract?

where is the boy?

and the mother?

the mother was screaming

she gave birth blindfolded

she never held him

they left her an old cellphone

somewhere not in Shanxi

the mother imagines
her son's a pit pony
searching smouldering coal seams
for her

bird song

in Tokyo
they're certain numbered cranes
paper bones
arranged in flight

in Canberra
they're doves
the first narrators
in the eye of God

in New York
they're cloth pigeons
the recipients
of invisible mending

in the Congo
they're parrots
flames of faces
in the rainforest

in Myanmar
they're swallows
feathers of prayer
in the mosque

in Bristol
they're starling figurines
decorated with silence
on a village green

at the Last Post
every bird airbrushed by war
raises a bugle

lament

we flew past shame-faced
cattle trains we flew past
the mountain range of bodies

we flew past the book-keeper
sorting foreign money

when we flew past the chimneys
stars of ash clung to our legs
small sad postcards
of where we'd been

after my father

after my father read *Hansel and Gretel*
he never left me in the forest
or anywhere near
his busy factory chimneys

he was a true father
who obeyed his boss
a loving father
who kept German shepherds

some nights he counted stars
once when there were over two thousand
he tried to explain
how easily they turned to ash

from the top step of the slide
in our villa garden
I used to wave to the many trains
that hurried to his factory

my father told me
all those screams and gunshots
were only kind engineers
protecting families from wolves

wolves were everywhere

now the swallows pilot planes

when they used carts
soldiers stole their paintings
and loaded their families
into trains

when they used boats
they were sold craft
that overturned and the world
called them refugees

now the swallows pilot planes
of dark blue feathers
their flight path above
the sky's commercial stomach

above shadows of skyscrapers
in a clearing where they wait
with a compulsion
never fully understood

if you look

there is something held
by more than physics
in this rough air above Verdun

the souls of soldiers
some still on horseback
float in the arms of angels

the last carrier pigeon
787-15
stunned by gas and fumes again

and again draws fresh air
from the release loophole
in Raynal's command post

and delivers his message
difficult to breathe
and falls into the field

of bone smoke shellfire
until the wind
the shadow of larger wings

raises the brave bird
beyond Cathédrale
Notre-Dame de Verdun
beyond tomorrow

beyond the wire

they leap through windows
and off roofs in Afghanistan
in Syria in Iraq

they cross borders
and walk beyond the wire
through dry riverbeds

open corn fields
dusty deserts to prepare
paths for their masters

though their olfactory bones
are paper-thin they do
rapid sniffing and lead

the way onto battlefields
to find improvised
explosive devices

there are photographs
of army and air force
staff sergeants learning

canine CPR and the symptoms
of canine post-traumatic
stress disorder and cuddling

and rewarding their dogs with toys
and there are photographs
of the same masters

limping across tarmacs
carrying their dogs
in blood-stained canvas

as carefully as flags

in Waiōuru the call to worship

where stars hold their breath
the forest is lantern lit
the altar makeshift

the Padre now commander
welcomes new soldiers
with the sign of peace
his lesson the road home

my son checks his right thumb
now a highway of white heat
he'd ignored a warning
and touched his gun's barrel

now he walks forward
with the mag 58
rests it on the bipod
the way things are done

though in this clearing
the earth is less bruised there's blood
when the Padre breaks bread

so my son receives
more than an order
more than anything

my mother darned the windsock

my mother darned the windsock
she grew up near
the Rongotai Aerodrome
her house never touched the ground

my mother delays flights
by feeding birds near the hangars
and loitering in restricted areas
especially the runway

when planes bring soldiers home
she's always there with the flag
of Aotearoa
broken-hearted like any mother

waking the waka

Rewa shifts the hull
of the sea with her breathing

her throat fills
with marine voices   *they're waking the waka*

her lungs flood with spume and
propel waves like paddles   *they're washing the waka*

my mother remembers
Tahu's return from Afghanistan

his sealed coffin so small
it made my mother recoil
she could never tell Rewa

through the window my mother
watches the great canoe   *they're dressing the waka*

then Tahu as tall
as the man he was
parts harakeke and toetoe

opening the spirit pathway   *blessing the waka*
for his mother

inside	**outside**
we are good children	we sleep in blown-out buildings
we do their cooking	the stars our ceiling
we carry their babies	we lose our brothers
from the back kitchen	we'd run if we could
we defend their houses	from shrapnel from explosions
no one looks for us	we cannot see the sun

endangered

1 bring into danger
expose to harm

2 from hunters / from
nets / the ways of water

3 from ash
and smoke / they begin to choke

4 feather voices forest voices / voices
that build / then forget

gifts

smoke

from arable waste
and illegal crop burning
the sky darkens
we were promised light

dust

from construction sites
moons of dust
clogs our lungs
the stars we pray to

exhaust

from millions of cars
we cough and choke
the fumes never stop
stealing our years

smoke and hair

On Ching Ming Day
she cycles through Shengfang smog
and the forests of buildings
to her mother's grave
even her fishing lamp stutters

last year she could hardly see
her mother's coffin
on that tricycle
for coal-laden fumes
she could hardly breathe

she wipes the headstone
her handkerchief blackened
like her mother's name
like the darkness where her mother
grew a teratoma

the cyst filled with smoke and hair
she hoped would be a sister
at the crematorium
her mother became industrial
and didn't recognise her

she cycles towards home
her plait forlorn and gritty
today in Shengfang
everything's shut down
even though it's spring

cold as not just ducks

cold as not just ducks
cold as tubes of oil look closer
tubes of feathers tubes of wings

pilgrim birds the river knew
devoted to water
birds the river called huia pīwakawaka

kākāpō kōtuku birds now sculptures
on a tree stump where they fell
upside down sideways twisted beaks open

beaks closed eyes open
eyes closed legs twisted
legs broken metal cold

much colder the river
under clumps of algae
mouth closed

seal pups picked like snowdrops

the morning none
of our babies woke
not even the sea hid them

we found the hammer
and their blood
on the frozen fingers of snow

we found their pelts
some with natal hair
flung over rocks

some of them we hadn't
taught to swim

some of them
we were still feeding

some of them
we've never held

Adelie penguin colony eastern Antarctic

through field after field of rising ice
a mother penguin drags the thought
of her chick like a cross

today fish are much further away
today there's hardly any

she returns home along the beach
past thousands of chicks
whose faith in hunger

wasn't enough to keep them
waiting for food

under the pavilion of the wind
she finds her own chick
between the feet of his father

as still as a circle of stones

from the Hutton's Shearwater
(*Puffinus huttoni*)

we turned
from the lantern
of stars
that kept us honest

and exchanged
the breath
of seals
of whales
for Kaikōura

and exchanged
the cape of fog
for the arms
of streetlights

who can say
they have never
left their wings
at the door
and followed
a lamp

like a promise
like something found?

reindeer roundup

now his mother
is a frozen pelt
strung between two poles
his name remains on her lips

inside the ger the herders
fry venison steaks
and stockpile hides and antlers
from the reindeer roundup

soon they'll be dancing
and toasting Christmas
the deer spreads his hooves
to stop sinking
the sky lowers like glass

when the music starts
in this northern wasteland
the deer remembers walking
on the village lake

and coming upon visitors
in the fragile tundra
instead the forest
is an abattoir of bones

the deer pauses
in the bruised snow
under that clump of lichen
the scent of his mother

Hokitika workhorse

when night falls
our hotel leaves her glass
and rises skyward

men in other rooms wrestle stars

I cannot guess if their shirts
have boatsheds or pineapples

by the time the sea arrives
we swim in sleep

I forget I had a horse
I forget I even worked

until the tide turns industrial
and a worried pit pony
hands me the reins

the taxidermist can't leave limbo

he sleeps awake with his exhibits
it's freezing outside he opens the curtains
is that the elephant standing in snow

her twin-domed forehead her arched back
she shouldn't have been taken from the forest
or made to carry a howdah

she shouldn't have
been executed
he looks again

is she kneeling
is she blindfolded
he could never

take India out of her
the swirl of sari the sacred Ganges
still floated in her eyes the ones

he replaced with prosthetics
he shouldn't have suspended her
between life and death

chemically altered in preparation
for the afterlife as an exhibit
but the taxidermist has children

and now must open the door
to a man cradling a Chinese water deer
snowflakes on its tiny cervine teeth

refugee

1 a person forced to leave their home

2 chased out without
crops houses villages / who floats and
fills oceans rivers / the mud their soft
faces / their blood

3 burnt out / their
melted shoes / nothing left to lose / their
language who they were / up in smoke

they are found in the sea

the Mediterranean

threw a baby

cold as a seal

into shoreline waves

into dehydrated oil

I couldn't leave him

in that shell of a mortuary

when the winds

turn back to Syria

I will bury him

in a web of olive leaves

my world is the sea

my eyes the sky

my brothers are birds

they wear beaks

they wear feathers

they struggle to breathe

I call for my mother

try to stand upright

but the boat won't listen

bury me

in the pelt of trees

wick

from the flicker of a boat
in the Aegean Sea
they took the heart

they built a cross
a twisted pale blue beak

the sky they followed
still and blue like the toddler
carried ashore by a soldier

carried through our televisions
the terrible cries of his father

that cross and a bowl
of votive candles
in the chapel at Pembroke

every candle a voice
between wick and flame
a Syrian refugee

who never arrived

the bear

the bear was found just alive
in shoreline waves by a woman
lonely for her son

at the border
the authorities
not as humane

used loudspeakers
and the sirens on their cars
to frighten the bear

under UV lights
they destroyed his pawprints
then stamped his identity
documents not eligible

when the bear told them
he wanted a longer life

they shot the air
to scare him away

they built a razor-wire fence
to keep him out

now he's somewhere
between land and sea
they call him displaced

at Mass in Streatham

everything is Polish
even the wind trunk
and bellows in the organ's belly

the migrant plumbers
painters maintenance men
forget their masters
on London's skyline
forget their burgled bedsits

and made worthy
by the Eucharist
light votive candles
for mothers in Warsaw
mothers in Kraków

and feed the collection box
for nuns in Gdańsk nuns in Łódź
Stefan remembers Holy Week
in Poznań and the covered
statues in the Basilica

and imagines himself
a shrouded figurine
on a Holloway building site
who cannot ask for work whose
native tongue has fled to Poland

at Mass in Streatham
these lilies in Oxfam suits
grow the eyes of God

in Norwich the angel brings my husband

to avoid the world's attention
the angel fled Bulgaria
and reached Norwich
by following the lights

they never turned him away
or denied him permission
he was never part of a quota
or a financial burden
for who can weigh wings?

in Norwich the angel
brings my husband a lamp
so he can breathe
in the Fishergate apartments

he drains the Fens
to make my husband sure-footed

he takes my husband
to Stranger's Hall
so he'll always know kindness
and to Tombland
so he'll never feel empty

the angel knows
how to get weaving
sometimes he uses a cycle
to get to choir practice first
to flood the Cathedral with light

some nights when the angel
doesn't visit Fishergate
my husband imagines him
in the Mediterranean
at the helm
of an overcrowded boat

what
we
hear

sheet

while we sleep
our ice sheet rumples
and rumbles into position

stomach

the ocean's stomach
fills with plastic bags
she takes her last breath

after the explosion

after the explosion
that bloodied silver button
holds nothing together

tusks

angry chainsaws
cutting tusks like roots
how dark the sky

net

codfish island
a yellow-eyed penguin
suffocates in a net

market

at the market
a pair of bear's paws
$8

the war cemetery

the war cemetery
an alphabet of white crosses
a blood moon

forest

even in the forest
Rohingya orphans still hear
the screams of their parents

where will the fish sleep?

a. they never thought the sea

the sea climbed a tall ladder looking for a room
    in Ishinomaki

she flung full-grown ships over bath houses penthouses
    hilltop houses

and ripped-out windows sidekicked buildings left debris
    seen from space

Tokiko's mother lifting her sister Tokiko's mother
    wrestling water

Tokiko's mother not answering Tokiko falling with the tide

under the monkey-bridge shrine under the willows under
    the emperor's kind words

live-streamed from Tokyo

b. after the tsunami the diver

waves of ghosts red flags where they sank

waves of ghosts hollow bones of houses offices dried
    fish factories

waves of ghosts shrunken heads of marine birds

waves of ghosts some on single legs

waves he daily dives like a low sinking moon in search of
    his banker wife

    now six years
    now 2190 days

her last text
    our manager orders us
    to lie on the roof

any shadow could be hers any silence the space
    between her eyes

the *tick tick tick* of his tank flicks through this calendar
    their life together

even under the waves ghosts arrive without her and
    hang around him
and float into his arms kind like strangers

c. mother Mekong

the Laos fisherman crosses the Mekong on a wire he
    planted in the dry season

his feet flex and ripple like wings above the hungry river

he stops   and casts
at Khone Falls

his net tricks the biggest fish travelling to Cambodia
   Horse of the Mekong

the harness tightens
          here

no here
    and here

soon the fisherman's a web of gasping threads

a fine
  line
at the mercy
of toes and tendons
       steps
     of
   faith

until he greets soft eroded rocks the green plaits of vines
the mouth of his smoky stilt-house

where his children his wife his mother

and eight
    small
wooden bowls
thank the Mekong

d. the zoo was never an ark

men climbed the great domes and towers to bring back to
    Earth spires bells crosses

to melt into money to build a zoo

when the flood came priests told us the zoo was never an ark

on the news I saw a bear floating on a heat-pump a
    hippopotamus dead in a drain

I never saw the elephant or the little wooden steps that
    climbed her back

or the terrible steel hook of her keeper

I like to think an angel returned her to Kenya

to collect grey skin bones tonnes of ivory to build elephants

e. his rickshaw his home

the sacred monsoon in Kolkata makes him holy with waist-
    high water

water too heavy for the *glug glug* of wheels their rims
    spokes hubs in nets of rain

too heavy to drown the only rickshaw actually moving
    actually certain to arrive somewhere

when rupees are thrown down to him by those desperate
to check on someone

desperate for an ambulance he cannot save their coins

f. sanctuary

our father cut a trapdoor in the cork floor of our Venetian
stilt-house

then dropped a line and fed us the fish of Italy

the canal rose and fell like a wheel and in the shallows

where we could breathe we stood and sang our father's
water music

the shutters opened the birds stopped the oar-locks the
basilica stood devoted

our father found three greyhounds to keep us warm to fill
our house with grace

the night our father took his guitar to town a flood
collapsed our stilt-house

though now we live in other houses we always row
towards our father

g. that made Darwin proud

lime trees rise like abandoned corridors and lead to
    a river
where swans are loyal to the table do they mean
    water table?
do they mean Darwin left school for them?

boat sheds lean into water urging oarsmen to row like
    wheels turning industry
into natural history raising water like locks

aphids all beaks and no wings feast on the sap of lime
    trees to perfect as Darwin said
their survival their gift to future generations

a sudden helm wind and the oarsmen brace their feet
    against the stretchers
another strong gust and ribbons of salmon shrug on
    their silver coats of migration
and wave to the swans leaning boat sheds and aphids

and with the same urgency that made Darwin proud the
    lime trees
convinced salmon will return wave their heart-shaped
    leaves with looms of weaving aphids
and from the clothing of the ground the papery wings of
    their fruit

h. island of the eels

you explore the centre of the Fens and by the towpath
    where the waterways are lock-free

meet two eel-catchers closing the necks of their nets

they say to catch anything look at the river

there are places to sit

in the distance are fields of waving mustard and the
    lantern tower
of Ely Cathedral where your votive candle prays

when the curfew bell rings every swaying lamp
in the eel-catcher's stilt-house
reverts to water

i. from the Arahura River

he tickles a thick-bodied trout that throws itself

back to unveil the path of the Arahura River

what remains in his square hands?

bones of water enough to mix with shingle

river sand wild grass to grow a daughter

up on the steep riverbank his empty fishing kete

with soft shearwater feathers

and pāua shell eyes hooks the harvest moon

and through this folded darkness grasses blow the wild
    sands know

the spiral of his daughter in the headwaters

where the river weaves her bones a coat of greenstone

j. how they leave the world

on the merry-go-round polar bears cling to the reins

of cracking icebergs

each turn of the machine raises the sea

so the bears are forced to dance then surf

under the red lights they remind us of club hunting

under the ebony lights they remind us of oil

the fairmaster won't stop the merry-go-round

the sea from her greenhouse cannot lower herself and
    snatch the key

every day these bears in bubbles of blurry fur

quiver   drift
    dwindle   away

Acknowledgements

Thanks and appreciation for their support and encouragement to Bill Manhire, Fergus Barrowman, Spencer Levine, Ashleigh Young, Kirsten McDougall, Craig Gamble and Frankie McMillan, together with Christine Leighton, Rebecca Ball and Di MacDonald of St Andrew's College.

Acknowledgements are due to the following publications where some of the poems in *Louder* first appeared: *Sport*, *Snorkel*, *Landfall*, *Sweet Mammalian*, *London Grip*, *Atlanta Review*, *Pedestal Magazine* and *Takahē*.